D0107665

Christina Kirk and Thomas Jay Ryan in a scene from
Suitcase or, Those That Resemble Flies from a Distance.

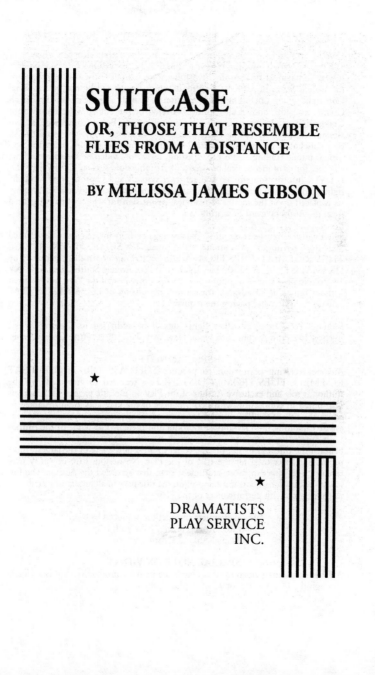

SUITCASE
OR, THOSE THAT RESEMBLE
FLIES FROM A DISTANCE

BY MELISSA JAMES GIBSON

DRAMATISTS
PLAY SERVICE
INC.

2

AUTHOR'S NOTE

About the architecture: Primarily, we see a significant portion of an apartment building's stairwell and two of the apartment doors to which it leads; we also see parts, fractions really, of the interior of two apartments, inside of which should be evidence of the women's dissertations in progress. Perhaps Sallie's apartment also features makeshift furniture fashioned from the arrangement of books.

About the language: The line breaks, internal capitalizations and lack of punctuation in general are intended as guidelines to the characters' thought processes, in terms of emphasis and pattern; they should be honored, but not enslaving. The cadence should fluctuate according to circumstance and should avoid falling into repetition. The rhythm of the piece as a whole should reflect the momentum of active thought. By extension, during the play's many transitions, solutions other than blackouts should be at all costs sought. Moments should not so much cut in and out as deftly replace one another. The scene titles, which appear in bold in the text, may or may not be projected or otherwise included in production.

About "/": When a backslash appears in the text, it indicates that the next line should begin, creating an overlap with the previous line.

SUITCASE OR, THOSE THAT RESEMBLE FLIES FROM A DISTANCE was originally produced by Soho Rep (Daniel Aukin, Artistic Director; Alexandra Conley, Executive Director) and True Love Productions in New York City, opening on January 24, 2004. It was directed by Daniel Aukin; the set design was by Louisa Thompson; the costume design was by Maiko Mattsushima; the lighting design was by Matt Frey; the sound design was by Shane Rettig; the original music was by Michael Friedman; and the projections were by Elaine J. McCarthy. The cast was as follows:

SALLIE .... Christina Kirk
LYLE .... Thomas Jay Ryan
KARL .... Jeremy Shamos
JEN .... Colleen Werthmann

CHARACTERS

SALLIE, 30s
LYLE, 30s
KARL, 30s
JEN, 30s

SETTING

The play takes place in present-day New York City.

These ambiguities, redundancies, and deficiencies recall those attributed by Dr. Franz Kuhn to a certain Chinese encyclopedia entitled *Celestial Emporium of Benevolent Knowledge*. On those remote pages it is written that animals are divided into (a) those that belong to the Emperor, (b) embalmed ones, (c) those that are trained, (d) suckling pigs, (e) mermaids, (f) fabulous ones, (g) stray dogs, (h) those that are included in this classification, (i) those that tremble as if they were mad, (j) innumerable ones, (k) those drawn with a very fine camel's hair brush, (l) others, (m) those that have just broken a flower vase, (n) those that resemble flies from a distance.

—Jorge Luis Borges
"The Analytical Language of John Wilkins,"
Other Inquisitions, tr., Ruth L. C. Simms (1964),
Austin: U. of Texas Press, 1995, p. 103

SUITCASE
OR, THOSE THAT RESEMBLE
FLIES FROM A DISTANCE

EXPOSITION

Jen, Karl, Lyle and Sallie sing.

LYLE
THIS FUNNY FEELING'S REALLY NOT THAT FUNNY

SALLIE
HE SAYS HE'S NEVER KNOWN A NOSE THAT'S QUITE AS
RUNNY

JEN
I WONDER HOW WE WERE BEFORE WE WEREN'T

KARL
SHE SAYS I'M PRONE TO THOUGHTS THAT ARE NOT
CURRENT

SALLIE, JEN, KARL and LYLE
(Chorus:)
SOME WORDS ARE HARD TO SPELL

SALLIE and JEN
(said)
Fahrenheit

SALLIE, JEN, KARL and LYLE
SOME WORDS ARE PROBLEMATIC

KARL and LYLE
(said)
Titular

SALLIE, JEN, KARL and LYLE
SOME WORDS SOUND BETTER IN
OTHER TONGUES
AND LONGING IS A SEVEN-LETTER WORD

KARL
WHY DO HUMANS FEEL CONTEMPT FOR HUMAN
ERROR

LYLE
WHY IS SHE HERE WHILE I AM ALWAYS THERE

JEN
IS THIS HOUSE OF LOVE JUST BRICKS WITHOUT MOR-
TAR

SALLIE
I SHOULD HAVE BEEN A DOCTOR WITHOUT BORDERS

SALLIE, JEN, KARL and LYLE
SOME WORDS ARE HARD TO SPELL

SALLIE and JEN
(said)
Rhythm

SALLIE, JEN, KARL and LYLE
SOME WORDS ARE PROBLEMATIC

KARL and LYLE
*(said — Karl pronounces it "Yura-nus," Lyle pronounces it "Your
anus")*
Uranus

SALLIE, JEN, KARL and LYLE
SOME WORDS SOUND BETTER IN

WHAT RHYMES WITH MY GIRLFRIEND

In the vestibule. Essentially, Karl and Lyle are not welcome in their girlfriends' apartments, an awkward state of affairs that is reflected by the fact that, despite adopting a series of "relaxed" physical behaviors, neither one is able to get truly comfortable during the scene.

LYLE
Won't it be
Nice

KARL
(it's such an odd word when you think about it)
Nice

LYLE
when our girlfriends'
dissertations are
finished

KARL
My girlfriend's dissertation Is finished Boy
Is It Finished

LYLE
Oh my
girlfriend didn't mention that your
girlfriend's dissertation was
done

KARL
Oh no
my girlfriend's dissertation isn't

Done
my girlfriend's dissertation is
Finished

LYLE
My girlfriend said your girlfriend's
dissertation was about garbage

KARL
Garbage Detritus What Is Left My girlfriend
believes what we discard is of much
greater interest than what we keep My girlfriend
went through the garbage of three randomly
selected individuals over a period of
five years My girlfriend
essentially used the garbage as a means by
which to deduce identity or
construct identity depending upon your
point of view What's
your girlfriend's dissertation about

LYLE
My girlfriend's dissertation is an
examination of examples of alternative means of
storytelling by which my girlfriend
means for instance end-beginning-middle or
middle-middle-middle instead
of beginning-middle-end My girlfriend
feels that life actually
actual life feels
an affinity for Other Constructions My girlfriend's
dissertation is called Narrativus
Interruptus but I'm hoping my girlfriend will change it to something a little

KARL
more catchy

LYLE
less unfortunate

KARL
My girlfriend's dissertation is at
a standstill because of issues of ethics
because my girlfriend received permission from her
advisor to riffle through the garbage of
strangers but not from the strangers
themselves My girlfriend's dissertation has
thus itself become garbage has itself become
a prime artifact of her thesis and of course
though she's angry this also makes my
girlfriend laugh This makes my girlfriend
laugh a lot

LYLE
My girlfriend's dissertation is not
proceeding My girlfriend is in a
rut somewhat My girlfriend says
her advisor is not overly
happy with her My girlfriend is
not overly happy My girlfriend does
not laugh a lot

KARL
I bring my girlfriend
garbage gifts of
garbage The
garbage of three strangers

LYLE
Instead of focusing on her dissertation
my girlfriend focuses on the awkward encounters
she shares with her adviser For
instance she dwells on the time at her department's
holiday party when they were greeting and
misread one another's psychophysical signals
and wound up engaged in what was neither a
hug nor a kiss nor a handshake but some
bungled civilian amalgam

KARL
I enjoy bringing my girlfriend suitcases full of

garbage gifts of
garbage
offerings of unwanted love
unwanted offerings of love I
don't know what I mean

LYLE
My girlfriend has trouble
finishing things

KARL
My girlfriend's dissertation is
Finished
boy is it finished

LYLE
My girlfriend wonders why the world
embraces all things intellectually obvious

KARL
Tell your girlfriend all things intellectually
obvious are deeply lovable and in this age one
cannot argue with even remote lovability

LYLE
I did

REMEMBER OUR CROSS-COUNTRY
TRIP THAT TIME

*Beside Sallie's manuscript sits a lamp without a shade. Sallie
picks up her pen, stares at the manuscript and then puts down
her pen. Sallie unscrews the illuminated bulb and inserts
another she selects from a pile of bulbs. She is either testing the
goodness/burnt-outness of identical-looking bulbs or trying
out a whole array of different styles and colors of bulb at var-
ious points during the following scene. Meanwhile, Sallie and*

Jen talk on the phone. Meanwhile, Lyle and Karl loom in the building's vestibule.

SALLIE
What I was saying before it
depends on your orientation

JEN
Sexually

SALLIE
Directionally
It depends on which way you're
facing
Remember our cross-country trip that
time
That was something
Do you remember our cross-country trip that time Jen

JEN
Why

SALLIE
No reason
I was just thinking about how you
know on our
Cross-Country Trip That Time we were hungry to
See As Much As We Could
That's all I'm sorry I think I'm um feeling
ashamed of my stupid life

JEN
What

SALLIE
Ashamed
Sorry

JEN
Why

SALLIE
Oh
My
Stupid Life I'm
Ashamed of it
It's just that when I was younger I wanted to see everything Do You
Know What I Mean
I wanted to See Everything
But now I find I
basically go through My Stupid Life um
averting my eyes
basically
Do you avert your eyes Jen because
I avert my eyes Jen I
avert my eyes and the
list of things from which I avert my
eyes Jen is um
Big
And getting um
Bigger and that Feels Wrong
Are you there

JEN
I'm here

SALLIE
Oh you're there/ good

JEN
Yes

(Karl enters and buzzes Jen's apartment: buzz.)

SALLIE
Do you think that's Wrong

(Buzz.)

JEN
(speaks into intercom as she continues to hold phone)
Yes

SALLIE
You do

(Buzz, breathing.)

JEN
Yes

SALLIE
See I do too but then I was wondering
Is that the right word Wrong
Is Wrong right or um fair to one when one is simply reporting
one's emotional response —

(Makes it plural on second thought.)

— ses

(Buzz.)

JEN
Who is it

SALLIE
Are you/ talking to me

KARL
It's me

JEN
Who's me

KARL and SALLIE
Me

KARL
But um

SALLIE
In any case the list is long
I mean Big I said Big before I

17

KARL
But um

SALLIE
That's all I'm basically saying

KARL
(I feel suddenly unsure of your name)
But um NnnnSsssWw-wwLllll

LYLE
Lyle

KARL
Lyle's here

JEN
Why

SALLIE
No reason

KARL
He just is

SALLIE
No defensible reason

LYLE
Hi Jen

KARL
He just is

LYLE
Hi Jen

SALLIE
But lots of defensive reasons ha ha

JEN
What

SALLIE
Nothing

KARL
Hi Jen

LYLE
Hi/ Jen

KARL
Hi/ Jen

LYLE
Hi/ Jen

JEN
Right

(Lyle suddenly approaches the intercom.)

LYLE
(to Karl)
May I
Super quick thing

(Cough, into intercom.)

Jen

JEN
Pardon

SALLIE
What
Nothing

LYLE
Sorry

19

JEN
Why

LYLE
I coughed

SALLIE
Sorry

JEN
Why

LYLE
I/ coughed in your ear

KARL
He coughed

SALLIE
Oh
I don't want to talk about it

LYLE
Okay I have a question/ Have you spoken to
Have you spoken to

JEN
Okay

KARL
I have a question
I have a question
I have a question

(Specifically to Lyle, softly and with a gesture.)

to pop

LYLE
Oh
Okay

Uh okay
Karl has a Question

(Lyle moves away from the intercom.)

Ask her

(Buzz. Pause.)

KARL
Did we/ lose her

SALLIE
I'm sorry

KARL
Did we/ lose her

SALLIE
Are you/ there

LYLE
(pronounces the "n" in damn)
Damn it

JEN
I'm here

KARL
Oh/ she's there

SALLIE
Oh you're there/ good

LYLE
Good

KARL
She's there

21

LYLE
Ask her

JEN
What

LYLE
(pronounces the "n")
Damn it/ man

JEN
WHAT

LYLE
Take charge/ of yourself

SALLIE
You mean like what things

LYLE
Karl Jen has a Question

JEN
Uh huh
I'm listening

LYLE
I mean I'm
sorry it's none of my

(Unfinished sentence:)

It's your

(Finished sentence:)

It's his

(Lyle retreats. There is suddenly nothing between Karl and the intercom except Karl himself.)

JEN
Hello

(Somewhere during the following Karl hiccups.)

SALLIE
Um okay Petitions I avert my eyes from um
Political Petitions and I avert my eyes from
Personal Grooming Well
especially Personal Grooming in Public so uh
Public Personal Grooming you know

LYLE
What's wrong with you

JEN
Me

SALLIE
Excuse me

LYLE
Him

(Karl hiccups.)

JEN
What's that sound

LYLE
What/ sound

SALLIE
It's the sound of me telling you things Jen things/
from which I Jen avert my eyes

(Karl hiccups.)

JEN
That sound

LYLE
Oh Karl has the hiccups

(Karl nods.)

See he just nodded

JEN
Oh

KARL
Could you

(Karl hiccups.)

LYLE
Could I what

KARL
Could you

(Karl hiccups.)

LYLE
I don't understand

KARL
Could you

(Karl hiccups.)

you know

LYLE
Oh
please don't tell me you're asking me to ask her You should/ ask her

KARL
Please just

(Karl hiccups.)

LYLE
You/ should

KARL
Please/
Please just

(Karl hiccups.)

Please just

(Karl hiccups.)

LYLE
You should Okay Okay Okay

(Into intercom.)

Will you marry him

SALLIE
I also avert my eyes from um Pain

JEN
What

LYLE
Will you/ marry him

SALLIE
Pain

(Karl hiccups.)

JEN
What does that mean

SALLIE
Oh People's Pain
I guess I'm randomly starting with the P's

25

LYLE
Can he be your husband

JEN
Oh

LYLE
No

JEN
OH

LYLE
(to Karl)
Oh

(Karl hiccups and indicates through gesture a question:)

Karl is wondering what Oh means

SALLIE
As if anything's random right But
I avert my eyes from things that start with uh
tons of different letters Jen Tons of different letters

JEN
Uh huh

LYLE
Karl wonders is that A Yes
Will Karl be able to refer to you as wife

JEN
Are you kidding

SALLIE
Well Tons is hyperbole sure but the point is I avert my eyes from
Far Too Many things

(Karl hiccups.)

LYLE
I don't mean Address you as Wife
I mean in conversation like My
wife and I just saw this really disappointing uh movie Things
like that

(Karl gestures and hiccups.)

Oh Karl's trying to say something

SALLIE
Sometimes I stand at my window Jen and I can't tell if
it's bleak in here or bleak out there or
both Do you know what I mean

(Pause. We start to see flickers of light emanating from the window across the street. Sallie doesn't notice it yet; instead she puts the phone down and contemplates her stupid life.)

JEN
Are you there

KARL
I'm here I've brought something

JEN
What is it

KARL
I've got Lyle here

JEN
Lyle is someONE

KARL
Yes I know I said the wrong thing I've
got Lyle here

JEN
Yes I know I didn't know you knew Lyle

KARL
I don't Have you got Sallie there

JEN
What do you mean
I'm here and Sallie's at Sallie's
Sallie's there but she's not here Karl

KARL
Lyle's brought her something

JEN
Something for Sallie

KARL
He sends his love

JEN
You're forwarding Lyle's love

KARL
I'm delivering it

JEN
You're working together

KARL
Why not

LYLE
Can he come in

KARL
Can I

LYLE
Can he

KARL
Can/ I

LYLE
Can/ he

KARL
Can/ I

LYLE
Can/ he

JEN
Hmm
hon
hmm

(Sallie stares out the window.)

SALLIE
All I'm saying is Remember Our Cross-Country Trip That Time

(Jen opens a suitcase and pulls out a bag of trash. She opens the bag of trash and pulls out a late 1960's era cassette tape player. Then, she finds several cassette tapes among the garbage in the trash bag. Jen stares at the cassette tape player while Sallie stares at her dissertation: a huge stack of paper. Jen picks up one of the tapes and inserts it into the cassette tape player. She presses the recorder's "play" button: The tape seems to be blank. She takes the first tape out and inserts another one. She presses "play" again. Tape excerpt #1:)

JEAN
It lights up.

PETER
It does?

JEAN
Doesn't it light up, Gene?

GENE
Yes, it lights up.

PETER
Cool.

(Jen presses "stop," examines the tape and realizes it hasn't been fully rewound; she presses "rewind" and then "play." Sound of breathing in the forefront, Christmas music and the family unwrapping presents in the background.)

LIZZIE
Okay, so …
Daddy.
Daddy.
Daddy.
Daddy.
Daddy.

GENE
What?

LIZZIE
It's not working.

GENE
What?

LIZZIE
My present's broken.

(Slight pause. Breathing again in forefront.)

Daddy.
Daddy.
Daddy.

GENE
What?

LIZZIE
The tape recorder's not working.

GENE
It's not? Yes it is, see? The — what are those knobby things called?/
— heads are turning.

PETER
Heads.

LIZZIE.
Oh.

(She clears her throat.)

You are my new Sony Series Two tape recorder.

(Sound of breathing.)

I love you.
Mommy's opening her present.
Everybody's here.

PETER
Can I open one?

(Sound of breathing, unwrapping.)

JEAN
Oh, this is great.

LIZZIE
Mommy got a coat of brown and beige squares and rectangles and
she says it's great.

(Sound of unwrapping.)

PETER
Cool.

LIZZIE
Peter got a globe.

PETER
Thanks.

LIZZIE
It lights up.

PETER
It does?

JEAN
Doesn't it light up, Gene?

GENE
Yes, it lights up, Jean.

LIZZIE
Mom's Jean with a J, dad's Gene with a G.

PETER
Cool.

LIZZIE
Peter got a cool globe that lights up. It's so cool. And now I'm going to open up my puppy!

JEAN
You know it's not a puppy, hon.
Daddy's allergic.

(Sound of unwrapping.)

PETER
Dad, I think it needs a special bulb.

JEAN
That wasn't included?

LIZZIE
Oh, look everybody …
I got a pocketbook.

JEAN
I thought that was supposed to be included. Gene?

LIZZIE
I got a pocketbook.

JEAN
Gene, wasn't that special bulb supposed to be included?

LIZZIE
I got a pocketbook.

GENE
I don't know, Jean./ I suppose it

LIZZIE
I got a pocketbook.

JEAN
I thought you checked/ that.

GENE
I didn't.

JEAN
So I guess we won't be able to see it lit up, that's all. I'm sorry your father ruined/ Christmas, Peter.

GENE
We can get a/ bulb, Jean.

LIZZIE
I got a/ pocketbook.

GENE
Jesus.

JEAN
Say sorry, Gene. Peter, your father forgot to check to see if it came with a/ special bulb, so we won't be able to see it lit up.

GENE
Oh, for God's sakes, woman, if you say special bulb one more/
time.

LIZZIE
I got a pocketbook.

JEAN
Well, you said you'd take care/ of it.

GENE
I don't see a piano tied to your ass.

JEAN
WHAT did you say?

LIZZIE
And that's all the presents.

GENE
You heard me. You could've gotten the light bulb your/ self.

JEAN
You said you'd do it./ I'll take care of it, Jean. I'll take care of it,
Jean.

PETER
Are you recording?

LIZZIE
It's mine.

PETER
I'm just looking.

LIZZIE
So, okay,
That's all for now. Merry Christmas.
I love you, my new Sony Series Two tape recorder.
I forgot to tell you I'm Lizzie and I'm eight and I LOVE you —
oh, I did tell you that.

PETER
Say the date.

LIZZIE
December 25th.

PETER
No, dummy, the year.

LIZZIE
Merry Christmas, 1973.
Why?

PETER
So you'll know. When you go back to listen to it.

LIZZIE
I wanted a puppy.

JEAN
For chrissakes, Gene, were you too busy to take the time to read
the box? This is what I'm talking about. Children get disappointed.

LIZZIE
Did you want a puppy?

GENE
They don't seem disappointed to me.

PETER
I wanted a dog.

LIZZIE
I wanted a puppy to sleep with me in my bed.

(Breathing on tape, over:)

GENE. Only one person seems disappointed to me, Jean, that's
how it seems to me, Jean. Jesus, Jesus, Jesus, Jean.

(Breathing. After a moment Jen presses "stop." She picks up a Sharpie,

writes on a label and affixes the label to the tape. Jen picks up the
phone and dials Sallie's number.)

IT IS UM NOT

Ring ring.

JEN
I forgot to tell you that Lyle sent his
love

SALLIE
I called you

JEN
So I can't speak first

SALLIE
You saw Lyle

JEN
Karl told me to pass on Lyle's love and then Lyle asked me to
marry him on behalf
of Karl

SALLIE
Karl proposed

JEN
What a word it's
absurd don't you/ think

SALLIE
Proposed

JEN
Uh huh

SALLIE
He proposed

JEN
Uh huh

SALLIE
What did you say

JEN
Nothing

SALLIE
Lyle's passing on his love now

JEN
I guess

SALLIE
Did Karl propose on behalf of Lyle

JEN
No/
but you know he would

SALLIE
Oh
Who

JEN
What

SALLIE
He who
In other words Karl would propose on behalf of Lyle or Lyle
would propose

JEN
Lyle Listen
were you happy when you were
little

SALLIE
Little

JEN
Little younger you
know what little means It's an
idiom were you/
happy

SALLIE
I can't remember I don't think
so but maybe I was Not unhappy I
was probably neutral Do you want me to say
no on your behalf

JEN
You had a neutral childhood No

SALLIE
Maybe No

JEN
No no to the proxy no You
must remember something about your child/ hood

SALLIE
Uh I remember playing with my brother in a long hallway
riding a tin car okay I
remember our first record player You
don't want me to say yes for you do you

JEN
No So you were happy sometimes

SALLIE
I guess when
things were involved So
what should I say for you

JEN
Nothing Things are fraught

SALLIE
Did you say/ fraught Nothing

JEN
I did say fraught I did say nothing I
Don't Want You To Speak For Me

SALLIE
Oh

(Slight pause.)

I don't really like people
touching my things
I mean okay

(Slight pause.)

Remember that housesitter I had that time who
touched some stuff I specifically
told him not to

JEN
I don't want to talk about/ him

SALLIE
It was really Really upsetting

JEN
Maybe he got confused/ Anyway

SALLIE
That's not what happened

JEN
you don't know what stuff he touched

SALLIE
Stuff was in different places Jen Stuff
was all over the wrong place

39

JEN
I don't understand some
stuff he Was allowed to touch while other stuff
he Wasn't

SALLIE
Help yourself to my food I said
Make yourself Comfy in my bed I said
Use my towel my soap my chair I said
Water my plant if you remember I said
If not it's really okay
Feel free to read my books I said
Even the ones with bookmarks in them
Remember to feed the cat I said
But anyway the cat will insist
Basically mi casa es su casa I said in
you know
Español
except please
Don't Touch This Stuff Here
And
of course/
Guess what he touched

JEN
He touched That Stuff There
He touched it all over the place
He smeared that stuff you told him not to touch
all over his/ body I bet

SALLIE
All right Jen all right I
don't need your your My
ability to envision Unpalatable Scenarios is plenty honed
Jen plenty
What I'm saying is I trusted the
housesitter with my Bookmarked Books and
I don't even trust the men I sleep with/ with my

JEN
(did you say)
men

SALLIE
man
with my Bookmarked Books No the
housesitter not only Disrupted stuff he Moved stuff to entirely
other places
places where
this stuff
had Never Been People
don't say fraught much anymore you know even
though people's lives continue to be fraught in the um/ extreme

JEN
Maybe you secretly wanted to sleep with
The Housesitter

SALLIE
The cat dish wound up in the cupboard and
my cereal bowl wound up on the
floor full of furry
water

JEN
How did you find him again

SALLIE
He was a stray

JEN
No the housesitter

SALLIE
Oh the housesitter I found the housesitter sitting on that slippery
slope
A Friend of a Friend

JEN
Friends of friends are never friends

41

you'd want for yourself

SALLIE
Yes friends of friends should befriend one another and enjoy one
Massive Tenuous Relationship It
would be easier for the rest of us

JEN
But aren't we someone's friend's friend

SALLIE
I REALLY CAN'T DISCUSS THAT RIGHT NOW JEN but
I will say this
The problem with housesitters is
they sit all over your house

JEN
And then there are all those friends of
friends of friends

(Slight pause.)

SALLIE
I didn't Secretly want to sleep with The House/ sitter

JEN
I Don't Want To Talk About Him How
is It going

SALLIE
(patting her dissertation)
You mean It

JEN
Um hmm

SALLIE
It is um not It
is not going
It is un-going/

JEN
It is ongoing/
It is ongoing

SALLIE
It is Un-going
It is UN-going
though you might say its un-going
is ongoing/ you might
say that Jen

JEN
Its un-going is ongoing

SALLIE
What's that/ Jen

JEN
You said I might say that
You said I might say/
Its un-going is ongoing

SALLIE
Oh
Oh
Haha I see haha so
How is It going for you

JEN
Um it is not as you
know It is not/
going
good

SALLIE
Aargh right

JEN
What oh
right aargh

(Small silence, in which they both feel silly for using the word "aargh.")

I was listening to a little kid's tape
before That's
why I was asking about your
childhood

SALLIE
What little kid

JEN
I don't know Lizzie
something
Lizzie X from the garbage of subject C

SALLIE
That sounds like a song sort
of/ Anyway

JEN
What

SALLIE
I should
What

SALLIE
Oh like
LIZZIE X FROM THE GARBAGE OF SUBJECT C

(Not singing.)

or something

(Pause.)

Okay I should
get back to It

JEN
Well okay I should well

I don't know what I should but
I'm so confused did you
want Karl to propose on behalf of Lyle

SALLIE
You're right that word is
Silly/ Do you

JEN
I said Absurd

SALLIE
What

JEN
Nothing

SALLIE
Do you think it's because of the
proximity of the two p sounds

(Slight pause.)

JEN and SALLIE
(hitting the two "p" sounds)
Propose

I SAID WHAT RHYMES WITH MY GIRLFRIEND

In the vestibule.

LYLE
You said Can he

(Points at himself.)

Be Your Husband She said

45

KARL	LYLE
Oh	Oh
You	You
said	hiccuped
What	What
You	You
said	hiccuped

KARL
Karl Is Wondering What Oh Means

LYLE
She said Uh Huh

KARL
You said Karl Wonders Is That A Yes

LYLE
(trying to remember)
She said

KARL
She said Are You Kidding

LYLE
No she said Are You Kidding in response to Will Karl Be Able To
Refer To You As Wife

KARL
Okay right so
what did she say in response to Karl Wonders Is That A Yes

LYLE
You know what Nothing She didn't have a chance because I
rephrased Karl Wonders Is That A Yes when I said
Will Karl Be Able To Refer To You As Wife

KARL
But that's no rephrasing Those questions aren't
at all the same thing

LYLE
I meant them as the same thing

KARL
You confused her

LYLE
Perhaps

KARL
Jen is so confused that Jen
is So Confused You Confused Her

LYLE
Sorry

KARL
(?)
Sorry

LYLE
Sorry

(A genuine silence.)

LYLE
Did you ever notice Karl how nascent bits of middle of the night
genius vanish without fail with the dawn

KARL
Holy Toledo Lyle and how
That Woman Is So Confused

DISSERTATION SHMISSERTATION

*Sallie sits in front of her manuscript reading and reordering
pages. Eventually, subtly, her revision process seems to border on
the random. Jen picks up another tape from the stack and presses*

"play" on the cassette tape player. Tape excerpt #2: different Christmas music playing in the background. Unwrapping is going on. Now thirteen, the girl is chewing gum as she speaks.

LIZZIE
Um, it's Lizzie.
So, so far Peter got a calculator, Jean with a J got a sweater,
Gene with a G got a book and I got a pair of pants with a belt attached.
Uncle Dick and Aunt Helene are here. They live in the Rockies.
Aunt Helene says it's God's country.
I've met them before, but it was when I was a baby, so I don't know them from Adam. That's what Aunt Helene said. We don't live in God's country.

SALLIE
(from her apartment, testing the word)
Propose
Propose
Propose

LIZZIE
(whispering)
Uncle Dick gets really drunk by about noon and then starts pronouncing e-ve-ry syl-la-ble he says real-ly care-ful-ly.

JEAN
(from the background)
Thank you, Helene, I just love it.

LIZZIE
Jean with a J just got another sweater.
She says she just loves it.

HELENE
(from the background)
Dick picked it out

(Sallie picks up the phone and dials Jen's number.)

DICK
(from the background)
We thought it would ac-cen-tu-ate your eyes

(Ring ring. Jen turns down the volume on the cassette tape player and answers the phone. Pause. Breathing.)

SALLIE
I don't think it is because of the proximity of the two p sounds Are
you
there

JEN
I'm here I thought
you might be my adviser

SALLIE
Ew there's a guy outside clipping his
toenails into the sewer Did
you hear from your adviser

JEN
She's trying to
Reach Me

(By now the flickering in the apartment across the way has resumed, attracting Sallie's gaze. She picks up a pair of binoculars and looks through them as she continues to converse. We see what she sees, a section of home movies circa 1940: A little girl, her father and her mother are sledding. The father wears a suit and overcoat, while the mother wears heels and a fur. They all take a turn on the sled.)

SALLIE
How do you know

JEN
She's left
Messages

SALLIE
Uh oh

JEN
And yesterday I received a
Letter

(Slight pause.)

Are you there

SALLIE
Sorry I got distracted Someone
across the way is watching some old
footage What did you receive

JEN
A letter Old
Footage

SALLIE
Home movies or
something What
sort of letter

JEN
She wanted to know where things
stood dissertation-wise

SALLIE
What did you tell her

JEN
It was a letter Sallie

SALLIE
(focused on the film)
Oh right
Isn't it beautiful Jen I mean is
there anything more beautiful Jen than
people who dress in blatant disregard of their
circumstances

JEN
Oh I don't know blatancy is problematic if you ask me Blatancy
makes me nervous She
said she was going through a messy divorce

SALLIE
Who

JEN
My adviser In her letter

SALLIE
That's too bad

JEN
So she's trying to straighten out her affairs so
to speak

SALLIE
So she can focus her energy on her messy
divorce

JEN
I guess She said attachment is a
nasty business

(Slight pause.)

That's a quote from her letter Attachment
Is A Nasty Business

SALLIE
(focused on film)
See I like blatant disregard It's got
what people used to call spunk

JEN
The rumor is her husband ran off with a grad student

SALLIE
Have you ever noticed how people who run off don't get any far-

ther than right in front of your face

JEN
I should call her

SALLIE
Do you know her

JEN
My adviser

SALLIE
Oh I thought you meant the grad student

JEN
Maybe a letter would be better Or a tape

SALLIE
A tape A
tape would be weird

JEN
Okay a letter

SALLIE
A tape would be weird

(Focusing on the film as the dad is sledding.)

Whee

JEN
What

SALLIE
Nothing

JEN
I should call her right/
away

SALLIE
Right

JEN
I'm going to call her Right Away

(Jen and Sallie hang up their phones. Instead of calling her adviser right away, however, Jen turns up the volume on the cassette tape player:)

LIZZIE
It's raining. My stomach hurts. I guess that's about it for now. Merry Christmas, 1978.

(Silence, except for the sound of breathing. Jen reaches over to shut off the cassette tape player but then we suddenly hear the girl's voice again, whispering:)

Last night I dreamed I was standing in front of a long clothesline of pieces of toast. All the pieces had a hole punched out of them and when you looked in each slice you saw a different miniature world. That's all I remember.

(Slight pause.)

Please, somebody, get me out of this house.

(The tape continues to play background Christmas noise for a few moments, before Jen presses "stop." Out the window the film is at the end of a reel. Sallie wanders back over to her desk and sits down. She sings:)

SALLIE
WHEN I WAS TWENTY
I GOT LOOKED AT PLENTY
AT TWENTY-NINE
THE WORLD WAS MOSTLY MINE
THEN THE TABLES TURNED
NOW I'M PRETTY MUCH SPURNED
AT THIRTY-THREE
I'M LOOKED AT MOSTLY BY ME
I NEVER KNEW

I'D COME TO PARTIALLY MISS
THE LOOKS I ONCE FOUND LASCIVIOUS

(Leaning over the cassette tape player:)

JEN
IN THE BACK OF YOUR PHOTOGRAPH
SEE RIGHT THERE
I AM THE ONE WITH THE
RECALCITRANT HAIR
YOU DON'T KNOW ME
'CAUSE WE'VE NEVER MET
A TRAGEDY FOR US
BOTH I SUSPECT
IF YOU'D TURNED AROUND
MAYBE YOU WOULD HAVE FOUND
THE ONE YOU DIDN'T KNOW YOU COULDN'T FIND
AND COULD YOU GIVE ME DIRECTIONS
TO THE BACK OF YOUR MIND

SALLIE
I'D LIKE TO BE THE PERSON

JEN
IN THE BACK OF YOUR MIND

JEN and SALLIE
PLEASE KEEP ME IN MIND

I SAW YOU NOD YOUR HEAD

Ring ring. Jen picks up the phone. Karl has his coat on but takes it off shortly after the scene begins.

JEN
Hello

KARL
It's Karl

JEN
Hi Karl

KARL
Okay I'm going to stop by

(Ring ring. Sallie picks up the phone.)

JEN
Shoot

KARL
What

JEN
I forgot I'm not answering the phone

LYLE
Sallie

SALLIE
Is this Lyle

LYLE
Yes
Did you forget to say hello

SALLIE
Yes
Hi Lyle

LYLE
I'm disturbed

KARL
Why Jen

SALLIE
Why Lyle

JEN
Because anyway
why Karl

KARL
Why Jen

LYLE
I was thinking about that map

SALLIE
That mat

LYLE
Map

JEN
Why are you stopping by

KARL
Oh because I want to talk to you

SALLIE
What mat

JEN
Oh

LYLE
Mappp

KARL
I want to talk to you about
you know

SALLIE
Oh map

JEN
Oh

SALLIE
Oh that map of/ your father's

KARL
You know

LYLE
My father's map
you know
the one from his most recent and possibly fatal trip

KARL
About your thoughts on
you know

SALLIE
Oh the map you found in your dad's car

JEN
I don't know Karl
I don't know if it's a good time to talk about

LYLE
that map

JEN
you know

LYLE
Of course That Map

(Pause. Breathing.)

KARL
Are you there

SALLIE
I'm listening

JEN
I'm here

KARL
My feelings for you are nothing to be afraid of but Jen
you know I have a policy

JEN
Oh right

LYLE
Of course that map

JEN and KARL
No feelings over the phone

LYLE
My father took a detour

SALLIE
What do you mean A Detour

LYLE
He'd marked the map with the most direct route

SALLIE
Yes we've been over this and over this
You think there's something nefarious about that

JEN
Still I don't know if you should come over Karl

KARL
My feelings for you mean you no harm Jen they're as benign as
could be

JEN
Benign feelings are the deadliest kind Karl Besides I'm not in the
mood for feelings Karl

SALLIE
Sometimes a detour is just a detour

LYLE
He'd marked the map Sallie

SALLIE
With the most direct route yes you said

LYLE
But his car was found twenty miles south of
the most direct route

KARL
I'm re-putting on my coat

JEN
But I don't feel like feelings tonight

LYLE
My father wasn't one to deviate Sallie
My father didn't Veer Off

JEN
Not just Your feelings Karl
All feelings Karl All
Feelings

LYLE
(pronounces the "n")
Damn it Sallie that wasn't his nature

JEN
Don't Re-Put On Your Coat Karl

SALLIE
Perhaps something struck his fancy
Something caught his eye maybe
Something or Some
One

KARL
You Never feel like feelings Jen

JEN
That's just not true

KARL
I've zippered up my zipper

LYLE
What's that supposed to mean

SALLIE
What

JEN
What
Unzipper your zipper Karl

LYLE
My father wasn't one to stray Sallie

SALLIE
Why are you speaking of him in the past tense
The past tense is so effing boring

KARL
Ew yuch

JEN
What

KARL
There's some old food in my pocket

JEN
Ew
Is it sticky

KARL
Sticky And wet

sort of

JEN
Ew

LYLE
The word effing is effing boring

(Pronounces the "n.")

Damn it Sallie
I'm sorry to effing bore you It's just
my father doesn't disappear

JEN
You can never get sticky stuff out

LYLE
Not every day anyway

KARL
I'd better change coats

SALLIE
It drives me crazy

JEN
You'd better throw out your coat

SALLIE
It drives me crazy that you pronounce the N in
Damn

LYLE
That's how it's spelt

(Pronounces the "n.")

Damn

KARL
Shoot

JEN
What

SALLIE
It's as bad as the effing past tense
It drives me crazy

LYLE
(pronounces the "n")
Damn

KARL
Shoot
I don't have another coat

JEN
Then that settles it

LYLE
I saw you nod your head

KARL
What

SALLIE
You saw me nod my head

JEN
You can't come over

LYLE
I saw you nod your head

KARL
When

SALLIE
When

JEN
Now

LYLE
Last week

KARL
I can still bundle up

SALLIE
When

JEN
How

LYLE
At the bakery

KARL
I'll wear layers

SALLIE
What bakery

JEN
That doesn't do me any good Karl

LYLE
The new bakery

KARL
What do you mean

SALLIE
Oh the new old bakery

LYLE
Of course the new old bakery

JEN
I mean whether you dress in layers or take off all your clothes

63

before you come over you'll still want to discuss
feelings aka you know when you get here
Won't You

SALLIE
What about the new old bakery

KARL
Nothing's changed if that's what you mean

LYLE
That's where I saw you nod your head

KARL
The fact that my coat has sticky and somewhat wet old food in the
pocket doesn't mean I've lost interest in discussing you know aka
my feelings
for you
with you Let's
stop saying aka okay

SALLIE
So you saw me nod my head so what

JEN
Well as I told you before
I'm not interested in feelings of any sort this evening

LYLE
The head pastry guy
was explaining the
chemistry behind unleavened bread
and You Nodded Your Head
When You Didn't Understand

KARL
I've got on three no
four layers

SALLIE
I don't understand your point but

SALLIE and JEN
Do me a favor

SALLIE
Don't Explain

JEN
Don't come over

KARL
I'm afraid it's too late

LYLE
I saw you nod your head is all
When you didn't understand

KARL
I'm on my way

SALLIE
Maybe your father wants to take a break from
you Lyle did you ever think of that Lyle because
lately Lyle
and I've been thinking about this
lately Lyle
talking to you is like eating
a hair omelette

KARL
I'm halfway out the door

LYLE and JEN
Nice image

JEN
but you're also halfway In the door Karl

SALLIE
When did you start taking emotional messages for Karl by the way
Lyle

KARL
What do you have against Karl's feelings Jen

LYLE
I have no idea what you're saying Sallie but this
isn't the conversation I pictured before I picked up the phone

JEN
Jen is begging you not to refer to yourself in the third person Karl

SALLIE
You picture your conversations Lyle

KARL and LYLE
I do it all the time

JEN and SALLIE
Let's talk in a little um
later on okay

KARL and LYLE
Fine

JEN and SALLIE
(?)
Okay

KARL and LYLE
I said fine

(Everyone hangs up.)

GREEK

Jen is sorting through a box of found garbage. Sallie is deeply involved in her dissertation — she's focused and appears to be having a burst of revision success right in front of our eyes. Then, her thought finished, she suddenly puts down her pen and picks

*up her phone. The phone rings in Jen's apartment. Jen answers
it. Meanwhile, throughout the scene, Lyle is sitting on the upper
steps of the stairwell, visible only from the shins down, his top
half in shadow. He might take off his shoe at some point and
remove a small rock from his sock and then put his sock and shoe
back on. Otherwise, he spends his time debating — from the
shins down — his next move.*

SALLIE
Tell me if this sounds pretentious but I'm beginning to
see my romantic life as alarmingly Aristotelian

JEN
When should I tell you

SALLIE
It's just that Lyle never does anything
inadvertent Jen He's so
intentional Jen He just doesn't
veer Is it too much to ask for
a partner who's capable of shunning purpose on
occasion I called my
adviser's voice mail

JEN
It's a good word though Aristotelian

SALLIE
and then hung up Sure but
try saying it fast three times

JEN
Why did you do that

SALLIE
Because I can't stop thinking about him

JEN
Aristotle

SALLIE
My adviser/ my adviser

JEN
Aristotelian Aristotelian Aristotelian

SALLIE
See

JEN
I thought you said he wasn't attractive

SALLIE
He's not but I Find him attractive

JEN
In what possible context would you find
yourself needing to say Aristotelian three times in a
row

SALLIE
Um say you felt like being
emphatic

JEN
Can you think of even one thing
you would characterize as being super-duper Aristotelian

SALLIE
Okay um
Life is hard for human beings
I am a human being
Life is hard for me

JEN
That was Aristotelian but I wouldn't say
it was super-duper Aristotelian

SALLIE
Okay well what if someone kept calling something
Platonic when it was actually Aristotelian

JEN
Uh huh and to correct this person you would just
sort of yell Aristotelian in his or her face
three times

SALLIE
Exactly

JEN
It's your adviser's power over you that you find attractive

SALLIE
I find his power over me annoying Actually
I find just about everything he does
annoying If he uses the word moreover in
conversation with me one more time I'll/ I don't know

JEN
So you find your adviser annoyingly attractive

SALLIE
I don't know I just want him to think I'm smart AND
admire my breasts

JEN
Have you ever tried to say Platonic three times fast

SALLIE
Or maybe I just want him to think my breasts are smart

JEN
Yeah but Sallie
at a certain point a person needs to
choose between looking good and accomplishing something
because it's just not possible to do
both

SALLIE
Platonic Platonic Platonic

JEN
That sounded much easier

SALLIE
It was

(Longish pause.)

JEN
One time when Karl and I first started
Ihatethatstupidphrase
seeing each other he called me up and said
It's Me before he was a me to me Do you
understand what I'm saying Sallie He
prematurely me-ified himself and it pissed me off

SALLIE
Wasn't it sort of flattering that he
wanted so badly to be a me to you

JEN
Me-ification should be offered not
taken Sallie

SALLIE
Shouldn't it be pissed off me

JEN
What

SALLIE
Sorry I'm just thinking about the split verbal whatever

JEN
You want me to say Karl's behavior pissed off me

SALLIE
Just if you want your annoyance to be
correct I mean it's your
call

(Slight Pause.)

JEN
Oh don't worry Sallie my annoyance is correct and
anyway
I'm not sure that that is in fact a split verbal whatever

(Karl appears at the intercom and basically buzzes every apartment, in response to which the building's misguided good Samaritan — every building has one — buzzes the stranger in without so much as a "who is it?")

SALLIE
Do you think that your adviser could beat up my adviser

JEN
Totally

(They each put down their phones without hanging them up. Sallie gets back to work, Jen gets back to sorting.)

SCENE IN THE STAIRWAY SCENE

Karl, appearing as a head, neck and shoulders, begins to ascend the steps as Lyle — feet, shins and knees — is prompted to stand up. Throughout the scene we hear a lot of that sound sandy grit makes when sandwiched between leather soles and faux marble stairs. For most of the scene Lyle and Karl are unable to see one another. In increments they will advance down and up the steps, respectively, so that by the end of the scene they have entirely reversed positions, with Karl seen only from the shins down and Lyle seen only from the neck up.

LYLE
Is that
Karl

71

KARL
(weird emphasis on "Lyle")
It's me Lyle

LYLE
I'm Lyle

KARL
I know you're Lyle I
emphasized the wrong word by
mistake

LYLE
I used to do that all the time

KARL
You stopped

LYLE
Let's just say I'm more
careful than I once was It's
hard to stop entirely How
is it out there

KARL
It's spitting

LYLE
Is it aggressive

KARL
The spitting

LYLE
Uh hmm

KARL
So-so

LYLE
Right I guess that's the nature of precipitation-type spitting as

opposed to expectoration-type spitting
which is almost always um

KARL
aggressive

LYLE
Yeah aggressive Once saliva leaves the mouth its functional aspect
turns ugly Anyway

KARL
It's raining a bit and
there's a chill in the air

LYLE
Ha in here too

KARL
What's that

LYLE
I said Ha in here too

KARL
But what does that mean

LYLE
It turns out my girlfriend's very anti-sigh We were
talking through the door and I
sighed as I stood there

KARL
Sighs have their place

LYLE
Sighs have no place for Sallie It turns out
she is um aggressively against sighs

KARL
They are funny things sighs Strange
beasts

LYLE
I don't know I just said what the eff
and left sort of

KARL
Semiverbal Semiphysical Sometimes signaling
deflation Sometimes signaling deflation's antithesis Strange
antithetical beasts sighs are

LYLE
Did I just say what the eff

KARL
Yes

LYLE
I meant fuck

KARL
But I will say this A full-blown sigh is a
corrective thing

LYLE
I just said what the eff Fuck and left
sort of

(As Karl/neck advances one step, Lyle/shins has lifted a shoe off the stair.)

KARL
So you know how when you said
Karl Wonders Is That A Yes
she said

LYLE
She said
nothing Karl

KARL
That's right she said nothing

(Lyle/shins examines the sole of one shoe.)

LYLE
Right

(Lyle/shins thinks "Aha, just as I suspected.")

KARL
and I'm not
saying no means yes Lyle but

LYLE
but

KARL
but
I might be saying nothing means yes

(Lyle/shins thinks "gum.")

LYLE
You think nothing means something Karl

(Pause, during which Karl/neck advances two or three steps while Lyle/shins attempt to scrape the gum off his shoe and onto the step. Perhaps, by the way, Karl had spit out his gum onto the staircase in an earlier scene.)

KARL
I think it's possible

LYLE
That Jen's nothing had content

KARL
That Jen's nothing was half full

(Both men sigh here, Karl's of the elated variety ["things are going good!"], Lyle's of the deflated variety ["you poor sad sack."])

LYLE
Well that's a really
gymnastic perspective Karl

(Pause.)

So here I go

KARL
Into the spitting chill

LYLE
I've got a warm coat

KARL
Myself
I dress in layers

LYLE
You're satisfied with that method

KARL
Ve/ry

LYLE
Really

KARL
Very
well it's new/ so

LYLE
Gotcha

KARL
we'll see

(Lyle exits the building.)

GESUNDHEIT

Sallie and Jen talk on the phone. Sallie sneezes.

SALLIE
So
How is / It going

JEN
Well/
It's not

SALLIE
Well
Well

JEN
Well comma It's not

SALLIE
Oh right

JEN
You

SALLIE
Same here same here Did
you write that letter to your/
adviser

JEN
Not yet but guess who I was just thinking about I was just thinking about that guy Ian

SALLIE
That guy Ian was in my dream

JEN
Really that guy Ian was in my dream

SALLIE
That guy Ian was in my dream

JEN
Really that guy Ian was in my dream

SALLIE
That guy Ian wanted very much to be my
boyfriend in my dream

JEN
Really that guy Ian Was my boyfriend
in my dream

SALLIE
Really
In your dreams

JEN
What

SALLIE
(hitting the "m")
In your dreaM
Anyway I don't know that
guy Ian thinks he's on film and
that guy Ian's not on film

JEN
Anyway the pertinent thing is in real life that
guy Ian doesn't give me the time of day

SALLIE
Because he thinks he's on film

JEN
But in my dreams that guy Ian
worships me

SALLIE
I'm here to tell you that he's not on film

JEN
And it's Extremely Disconcerting when someone who
formerly Had No Use For You Suddenly Does

SALLIE
Suddenly Does in your dreams

JEN
Still

(Slight pause.)

SALLIE
Monogamy's a bitch

(Slight pause.)

One time a group of us went to a bar after class and my adviser was
sitting next to me and I suddenly noticed our knees were touching
but I didn't know if he noticed our knees were touching and I did-
n't want to make a big deal movement that said Oh Our Knees Are
Touching And That's Socially Inappropriate Given The Confines
Of Our Relationship but in the meantime I had grown so focused
on the contact it felt like my knee was in fact throbbing so I decided
to conduct an experiment in which I would exert the smallest
degree of extra pressure to I suppose make the contact official but
instead I somehow lost control of my leg and basically wound up
knocking my adviser's knee with such incredible force that he
uttered a sound that can only be characterized as a yelp

JEN
Gesundheit

SALLIE
What

JEN
from before when you sneezed I

79

gotta go call my adviser

SALLIE
At this hour

JEN
Advisers don't sleep

IT'S FOR YOU

Sallie heads back to her dissertation and then shortly thereafter wanders over to her window, while Jen turns up the volume on the cassette player. Tape excerpt #3:

LIZZIE
Mom, I was listening to that.

JEAN
It's Christmas, Lizzie. At Christmas we listen to Christmas music. That's how you make things Christmassy. What's the point of Christmas if it's not Christmassy?

(Christmas music begins to play. As Jean walks out of the room she says:)

This'll get you in the mood.

LIZZIE
(ugh-type sound of frustration)
FA LA LA LA LA TO YOU, TOO, JEAN!

(Slight pause. For tape recorder's ears only:)

Do you see what I mean/ About everything?

(Sound of Lizzie breathing and Christmas music. Jen presses "stop" on the cassette tape player. Meanwhile, Sallie is once again at her window,

looking through binoculars at the neighbors' home movies. She and we see the following as the scene progresses: In this section of the home movies the family walks around a square, descends steps, and feeds pigeons. The girl wears a red coat and cowboy boots, with which she is obviously quite taken. The phone rings in Sallie's apartment.)

SALLIE
(answering the phone)
Hi Jen

LYLE
If we're/ speaking

SALLIE
Oh hi Lyle You're up/ late

LYLE
If we're speaking I want to say that in one's life there are only so many significant cusps Sallie

SALLIE
Significant cuffs

LYLE
Significant cusppps

SALLIE
Oh I was trying to figure out what a Significant Cuff would Be Maybe like on a bloodstained shirt at a crime scene or something

LYLE
If we're speaking that's what I wanted to say

SALLIE
I'm speaking Lyle Aren't you
speaking

LYLE
I'm speaking

SALLIE
I'm watching a little kid right now

LYLE
You're babysitting

SALLIE
No I'm watching a little kid out the window
who seems so happy who
thinks her cowboy boots will guarantee her
happiness because at this moment anyway they
define it
Things can be the authors of a fine albeit temporary happiness and
fine happiness of any length is hard to
argue with don't you
think Lyle

LYLE
Things need to be some other way is what I'm
saying if we're speaking Sallie

SALLIE
Are you trying to propose Lyle

(Pause.)

LYLE
Uh
n/ o

SALLIE
Oh

LYLE
You mean propose as in/ propose propose

SALLIE
No not nothing no

(Slight pause.)

LYLE
Not many people can pull off albeit

SALLIE
What does that/ mean

LYLE
You said fine albeit temporary

SALLIE
Did I

LYLE
When you were talking about the intersection of things and happiness

SALLIE
Oh well I don't like notwithstanding It conjures confusing imagery
I don't like it I just
don't

(Sallie takes the phone away from her ear without hanging up. She still watches out the window. Another home movie plays: The little girl plays a telephone game with her mother. We also see the girl's face in a sea of her dolls. We also see her receive instructions from off camera on how to pray. She prays. She sleeps.)

LYLE
I'm just saying you pulled off albeit so you know
Congratulations
Sallie
Sallie
Sallie

(Sallie hangs up the phone and dials Jen's number. The phone rings and Jen picks up.)

SALLIE
Do you ever wonder what
happens to all those little
girls at weddings who slide across the

floor in their stocking feet

JEN
They put their shoes on Sallie

I HAVE A POLICY

Sallie and Jen are still on the phone.

SALLIE
Lyle's dad tried to kiss me once

JEN
In a dream

SALLIE
In real life

JEN
But where is Lyle's dad in real life

SALLIE
Where indeed Lyle
perceives things selectively

JEN
Well Karl absorbs things slowly

SALLIE
He's not a paper towel Jen

JEN
I wonder

SALLIE
Wow
that's

abrasive

JEN
I'm not a cleanser Sallie

(Buzz.)

Hang on someone's at my
door

SALLIE
All right

(Jen presses "listen.")

JEN
Who is it

LYLE
(through intercom)
Lyle

SALLIE and JEN
Lyle

SALLIE
What's Lyle doing there

JEN
Hi Lyle what's up

LYLE
(through intercom)
Can I come up

JEN
No I said what's
up

SALLY
(through phone)
He wants to come up

LYLE
(through intercom)
No can I come up

SALLIE
Why does he want to come up

JEN
Lyle is something up

LYLE
Sort of

SALLIE
What did he say

JEN
He said Sort Of

SALLIE
What does Sort Of mean

JEN
In a way

SALLIE
I Know What It Means

(Buzz, beep.)

Hang on It's my other
Line

JEN
I'm still here

SALLIE
Hello

KARL
It's Karl

LYLE
What's up

SALLIE
Oh hi Karl

JEN
What

LYLE
Can I come up or
what

KARL
Can I come over

SALLIE
Can you hang on a sec

JEN
Just a second

SALLIE
Jen it's Karl

JEN
Karl why is Karl calling you

SALLIE
I don't know Where's Lyle

JEN
Lyle's outside He's
probably getting cold

(Buzz.)

KARL
Sallie

JEN
Hi Lyle

LYLE
I'm getting cold

SALLIE
Sorry Karl

JEN
Sorry Lyle

KARL
I need to talk

SALLIE
Can you hang on a sec

JEN
Crap

SALLIE and LYLE
What

JEN
I jammed my finger

SALLIE
What if we just spoke on the
phone Karl

LYLE
Ouch

JEN
I hate that

LYLE
It won't take long

KARL
See I have a policy

SALLIE and JEN
What's that

LYLE
What I want to talk about

KARL
No feelings over the phone

SALLIE
Wait a minute
He doesn't want to talk about feelings Jen

LYLE
It's about Sallie

JEN and SALLIE
What about Sallie

LYLE
It's cold out here

SALLIE
I'm going to ask Karl to break
his rule

JEN
Karl won't break his rule

SALLIE
Karl could you break your rule Karl

JEN
He won't do that
Sallie
Sallie are you there

KARL
Did you say something

SALLIE
Yes

KARL
I'm sorry
I dropped the phone

(Buzz.)

JEN
I'm here Lyle

LYLE
It's cold out here

JEN
I'm sort of um indisposed Lyle

LYLE
Do people still get indisposed

SALLIE
Do people still drop the phone

JEN and KARL
I do

SALLIE
Can you hang on a sec
Jen

JEN
I'll be right with you Lyle

SALLIE
What does he want

JEN
I don't know he's cold

(*Buzz.*)

JEN and SALLIE
Hang on

JEN
What's the story Lyle

LYLE
I'm looking for your perspective

SALLIE
I'm sort of indisposed Karl can
we do this over the phone

KARL
That's funny I was indisposed
just yesterday
Nevertheless my policy is no feelings
over the phone

JEN
Are you very cold
Tell me you aren't Very cold

LYLE
As much as I'd like to tell you I'm not Very cold Jen
the truth is I'm kinda cold Jen

SALLIE
You see I'm catching a cold Karl

KARL
Sorry to hear that Sallie Still
my policy stands

JEN
Try imagining you're stuck in an elevator without a fan

91

SALLIE
Karl could you break your rule Karl

LYLE
Without a Man

KARL
It's actually a policy Sallie it's not a rule

JEN
Without a Fan so that it's you know
Hot Anyway what is it you
wanted to talk about

SALLIE
Okay could you amend your policy Karl

LYLE
Sallie said something recently
something so

SALLIE
Pretty please Karl

JEN
What did Sallie say

SALLIE
Very pretty please Karl

KARL
Are you pressuring me Sallie

SALLIE
For me Karl

LYLE
It was something so

SALLIE
You can do it Karl

JEN
You can tell me Lyle

SALLIE
Come on Karl

LYLE
You know so

KARL
I don't like pressure Sallie
Pressure makes me FEEL upset oh MAN

SALLIE
Now that wasn't so hard/ was
it

KARL
That felt like a trick Sallie

SALLIE
Oh I'm not tricky Karl
Please don't think I'm tricky Karl

KARL
I had been hoping we could speak frankly

SALLIE
Sure thing

KARL
You know best friend's boyfriend to
girlfriend's best friend

SALLIE
Sure thing

KARL
Or whatever

JEN
Are you there

LYLE
All I can say is Sallie said something
so uh
That I guess I was hoping you could shed some light

JEN
I'll do what I can

LYLE
since everything gets filtered through my
own you know crap

JEN
Your own what

LYLE
My own you know
crap

KARL
Are you there

SALLIE
If you're asking me for advice Karl my answer is Sure Thing Karl
but keep in mind that whatever I have to say will have been filtered
through my own
you know crap

LYLE
I'm not like your boyfriend Karl

KARL
Your own what

JEN
(unwitting weird emphasis on "Lyle")
I don't have a boyfriend Lyle

94

SALLIE
You know crap

JEN
I mean I don't have a boyfriend comma Lyle

LYLE
You don't

KARL
Crap Crap oh sure your crap sure

JEN
In the sense that I hate that stupid word
All the language of attachment
I can't make heads or tails of it
Do you know what I'm saying Lyle

SALLIE
You still feel upset don't you Karl

LYLE
You mean you constantly find yourself deposited
in Russian novels you haven't read

SALLIE
I can hear it in your voice

LYLE
You mean most days you wake up and say Christ here
I am again on the train to effing Sverdlosk
I mean Catherinesburg

JEN
Uh
nooo not really Lyle

KARL
Of course I still feel upset
OH MAN I DID IT AGAIN

SALLIE
You're not going to drop the phone again are you

KARL
No but what's the point of a policy if no one
adheres to it

JEN
I mean I do have a boyfriend Lyle
I'm just saying I don't like the word boyfriend Lyle
In other words Karl's my boyfriend in every sense of the word
except the word itself you know what I'm saying Lyle
What are you saying Lyle

KARL
I mean my policy's not getting a lot of adherence here

LYLE
Wait
Did I just use the word effing

SALLIE
That's one way of looking at it

JEN
Yes

SALLIE
The other way is to see that you're just filtering through your
own you know crap

LYLE
I meant Fucking

SALLIE
Which is healthy

JEN
You sound upset

KARL
I wanted to get some advice from you Sallie but
here we are just talking about crap

SALLIE
Well don't take this the wrong way Karl but the
parameters of your policy kinda kill a phone
conversation

LYLE
Because it's not even a word

JEN
Effing

LYLE
I hate using words that aren't words

JEN
Well I wouldn't lose sleep over it

SALLIE
But anyway I know where you're coming from Karl I once had a
housesitter who sat all over my house and I'm still not over it
And speaking of crap try living under the curse of a cute
name

KARL
What are you talking about

LYLE
I'm sorry I'm a little on edge since my father's
Disappearance

JEN
That's right Where did he go

SALLIE
I'm
just trying to think of safe subjects here Karl I mean my hands are
sorta tied

97

LYLE
Well that's the problem isn't it

KARL
How do you spell it

SALLIE
ie not y

JEN
Oh right

KARL
Oh ie

SALLIE
My parents wanted it to be a little
Different

KARL
Mine wanted mine to be the same

JEN
So listen Lyle just tell me what Sallie said

LYLE
Right well we were discussing our future
essentially

JEN	SALLIE
(right)	*(how interesting)*
Uh huh	Huh

KARL
I come from a long line of Karlses I mean
Karls

LYLE
And I was expressing concern about you know the uh
status quo

SALLIE
How sweet

JEN
Uh huh

LYLE
Because I love her

SALLIE
I love long lines

LYLE
and because I hate her sometimes too

KARL
My son will be Dave

JEN
That's normal

SALLIE
A break in tradition

LYLE
And she thought I was on the verge of proposing
and I just find that so

SALLIE
Can you/ hang on a sec
Jen

JEN and LYLE
What

LYLE
's the word

KARL
Um sure

LYLE
So

SALLIE
Jen

JEN
What

KARL
Hello

LYLE
What

JEN
So what

KARL
Hello

SALLIE
Jen

JEN
SO WHAT
SO WHAT

LYLE
Oh uh
I see

SALLIE
Jen

JEN
WHAT

SALLIE
Karl's son will be Dave

JEN
What

SALLIE
Karl's son he'll
be Dave

JEN
Lyle

SALLIE
No Dave

JEN
Lyle

SALLIE
Lyle must be freezing

JEN
Are you sure Karl said Dave

SALLIE
Ask Lyle if he's dressed in layers

JEN
Not Dave-id

SALLIE
But don't tell him I asked you to ask

JEN
Lyle what are you wearing

SALLIE
And while you're at it askLylewhyhehasn'taskedmetomarryhimbut
don'ttellhimIaskedyoutoask

JEN
Lyle
Lyle

Lyle
Crap

SALLIE
What

JEN
Lyle left Just
Plain Dave

SALLIE
Karl definitely didn't say David I wonder
why Lyle left

JEN
I can't believe Karl's son will be Dave

SALLIE
That's so unlike Lyle to leave

JEN
I can't believe Karl's son will definitely be Dave

SALLIE
Something's up Definitely

(Jen and Sallie put down their phones. Sallie heads over to the window while Jen heads over to the cassette tape player.)

KARL
Um
Sallie

(Sallie picks up her binoculars and again watches the home movies playing in the apartment across the way: The family and extended family celebrate Christmas. The segment ends with the father writing "Merry Christ [new line] mas 1940" on the chalkboard the girl has received as a gift. Meanwhile, Jen presses "play" on the cassette tape player. The Girl on the tape is now a woman of thirty-seven. Tape excerpt #4:)

LIZZIE

Um, hello Sony Series Two. Guess who? It's me, Lizzie. Sorry I lost track of your whereabouts. That was rude.

Um, well it's been an uneventful couple of decades, I guess.

I did just get divorced.

Of course I keep trying to chart the road to my marriage's end.

Jean with a J was sad to hear it, but not surprised.

I was surprised to hear that she was sad and, um, sad to hear she wasn't surprised.

I trace it — the end that is, or the beginning of the end — to the moment when seemingly by accident we switched bedsides. Isn't that funny? He went away

for a week and each night I gradually moved my way over a little further and by the time he returned his side was mine. He didn't even mention it. I don't know.

It's all the

(Stumbles over the word.)

insignificancies

(Says it again, still gets it wrong.)

insignificancies.

(Says it again, still gets it wrong.)

insignificancies. I mean, isn't it?

Dad's mixing up some eggnog in the kitchen right now.

I don't think he knows what he's doing.

GENE
(from off)

Do you remember where your mother used to keep the baking soda, Liz?

LIZZIE

I guess that's about it. Oh, guess what I did? You'll enjoy this — I bought myself an early Christmas present. Guess what I got?

(Sound of unwrapping.)

103

I got … a pocketbook.
Merry Christmas, 2002

BUNGLED CIVILIAN AMALGAM

Lyle is on his hands and knees and is peering underneath Sallie's door. We hear the sound of grit meeting shoe as Karl ascends the steps; as he passes by Lyle he says:

KARL
Lyle

(Lyle doesn't move.)

LYLE
Karl

(Karl walks up one more flight.)

Sallie

(Karl knocks on Jen's door.)

KARL
Jen

(Karl knocks on Jen's door.)

LYLE
Sallie

(Karl knocks on Jen's door.)

KARL
Jen

(Karl knocks on Jen's door.)

LYLE
Sallie
(Karl knocks on Jen's door.)

KARL
Jen

(Karl knocks on Jen's door. Rest.)

KARL	LYLE
Jen	Sallie
Jen	Sallie
Jen	Sallie

(Jen is by now crouching on her side of the door, mirroring Lyle's position, although they crouch at different doors. In her apartment, Sallie stands facing the closed door with her arms crossed.)

SALLIE
Lyle

JEN
Karl

LYLE
Sallie

KARL
Jen

SALLIE
Lyle

JEN
Karl

LYLE
Sallie

KARL
Jen

SALLIE
Lyle

JEN
Karl

LYLE
Sallie

KARL
Jen

(Et cetera, until the reciting of the four names has accelerated to warp speed. Karl and Lyle suddenly get up and rush past one another on the stairway. As they do so, they say:)

KARL
Lyle

LYLE
Karl

(And then head to the outside of the other's girlfriend's door.)

KARL
Sallie

LYLE
Jen

SALLIE
Karl

JEN
Lyle

KARL
Sallie

LYLE
Jjjjjjennnnn

SALLIE
Karl

JEN
Lyle

KARL
Sallie Sallie

LYLE
Jjjennn Jen Jen Jen

SALLIE
Karl

KARL	JEN
Sallie	Lyle

SALLIE	LYLE
(I'm suddenly finding	*(I'm suddenly finding*
you a wee bit attractive)	*you a wee bit attractive)*
Karl	Jen
Karl	Jen
Karl	Jen
Karl	Jen
Karl	Jen
Karl	Jen
Karl	Jen
Karl	Jen
Karl	Jen

(More or less. Karl, unnerved, then rushes back to Jen's door and is surprised to find Lyle still there. Karl bends down in an incredibly awkward way — as opposed to just crouching — and whispers to Jen through the space beneath her door.)

KARL
Jen/

LYLE
Jen/

KARL
Jen/

LYLE
Jen/

KARL
Jen/

LYLE
Jenny

(Slight pause.)

KARL
Lyle

LYLE
Jen

KARL
Lyle

LYLE
Jen

KARL
Lyle

LYLE
Jen

JEN
Karl
Lyle
Karlyle

LYLE and KARL
Jen

(Ring ring. Jen picks up the phone.)

108

SALLIE
Jen

JEN
Sallie

KARL
Lyle

LYLE
Lyle Jen
Jen Lyle

SALLIE
Jen

LYLE
Jen

KARL
Jen

SALLIE
Jen

LYLE
Jen

KARL
Jen

SALLIE
Jen

LYLE
Jen

KARL
Jen

(Slight pause.)

JEN
Jen

(Slight pause.)

SALLIE
JEN

(Slight pause, calling through door.)

Kaarll

LYLE
Jen

KARL
Lyle

SALLIE
Kaarll

LYLE
Jen

KARL
Lyle

SALLIE
Kaarll

LYLE
Jen

KARL
Lyle

(Slight pause.)

SALLIE
(calling through door)
Lyylle

110

LYLE
Jen

KARL
Lyle
Lyle
Lyle
Lyle
Lyle

SALLIE
Lyylle

LYLE
Jen

KARL
Lyle
Lyle
Lyle
Lyle
Lyle

SALLIE
Lyylle

LYLE
Jen

(Silence. Breathing.)

KARL
Lyle

LYLE
Jen

KARL
Lyle

LYLE
Jen

KARL
Lyle

LYLE
Jen

KARL
(no it's)
Sallie Lyle

LYLE
Jen

KARL
Sallie Lyle

LYLE
Jen

KARL
Sallie Lyle

LYLE
Jen

KARL
(!)
Lyle

LYLE
(exactly)
Jen Lyle

KARL
(remember)
Sallie Sallie

LYLE
Sallie

(New idea.)

Karl
Sallie Karl

(In other words.)

Jen Lyle
Sallie Karl

KARL
(et cetera)
Jen Karl Karl Jen Jen Karl/ Karl Jen Jen Karl Karl Jen

LYLE
(et cetera)
Jen Lyle Sallie Karl Jen Lyle Sallie Karl Jen Lyle Sallie Karl

(During the above, pushing happens. Lyle falls down a flight of stairs.)

SALLIE
Jen

JEN
Sallie

KARL
Lyle
Lyle
Lyle
Lyle
Lyle

(Lyle stands up and walks up the flight of stairs with some difficulty, then turns suddenly to face Karl, who stands a couple of steps below.)

LYLE
Listen Karl, while I have no wish to add to any man's symphony of

sorrows, we must face the facts as they exist before us: Jen, for whatever reason — there may be one, there may be exponentially more than that — Jen does not find you winsome. Let me say it another way: your longing for Jen, Karl, is not pragmatic. As proof I offer the fact that Jen herself told me, and I quote, that she doesn't Have A Boyfriend Comma Lyle. In closing, I deeply regret that I am the bearer of this unwelcome news, although as such it should not surprise us, as most things that are pleasing are also by definition utterly, maddeningly elusive.

(Pronounces the "n.")

If you are so damn blind as to be unable to recognize the God's-honest-truth of the situation as I have laid it out before you, all I can say is Jeez Louise. In sum: you are wretched, you are undone, you are not Jen's boyfriend.

(Lyle promptly continues on his way up the stairs and back to Jen's door. Karl emits a guttural sound of suffering. He shoves his way past Lyle and hurls himself at Jen's door, attempting to break it down as he says the following and occasionally clutches his stomach. At the same time, Lyle sort of recoils in embarrassment for Karl and ascends the flight of stairs that takes him back to Sallie's door.)

KARL
I am the boyfriend of Jen
I am Jen's boyfriend Karl
I am Karl comma Jen's boyfriend
I Am Karl Comma Jen's Boyfriend
I AM KARL COMMA JEN'S BOYFRIEND

JEN
What are you wearing

(Karl is wretched; Karl rallies.)

KARL
Uh a T-shirt

JEN
And

KARL
A uh shirt

JEN
And

KARL
A uh 'nother shirt

JEN
And

KARL
Yet another one

JEN
No pants
No socks No
underwear No
footwear No
wrist watch No
um et cetera

KARL
Of course pants of
course pants and
all the rest These are
givens I thought
we were talking about
my top half I brought
you a suitcasefull of garbage for
old time's sake of
course pants I'm a
fan of pants I'm a
man of pants

JEN
Let me ask you something

KARL
Shoot

JEN
It's a non sequitur

KARL
Bring it on

JEN
You know that-guy-Ian right

KARL
Ian what's-his-face

JEN
Uh huh

KARL
Uh huh

JEN
Does that-guy-Ian-what's-his-face see anybody

KARL
What

JEN
Does that-guy/-Ian-what's-his-face see anybody

KARL
Why are you asking me if that-guy-Ian-what's/-his-face sees anybody

JEN
For a friend For a friend

KARL
Sal/lie

JEN
No/

KARL
Then/ who

JEN
Um that friend of my friend Kate who
only has friends who look just like her
I'm asking for/ Kate's friend

KARL
He sees everybody

JEN
What do you/ mean

KARL
Tell Kate's friend that that-guy-Ian-what's-his-face sees everybody
oh and Jen

JEN
Yes

KARL
Eff you

JEN
Eff me

KARL
You heard me

(Slight pause.)

JEN
Don't you think love should be more improbable

KARL
I don't know what that means

JEN
We're such a probable Ihatethisstupidword couple Karl

KARL
You think it's a problem that we're probable

JEN
It's a problem if love is supposed to be improbable

KARL
Why are only difficult things admirable to you

JEN
I don't know

KARL
Well I don't want to be forced to use the words juvenile romantic
and vision in close succession but

JEN
I'm complicated You always said you liked complicated women

KARL
Women who are complicated in a FUN way

*(Sallie is by now crouching on her side of the door, trying to peer
beneath it; Lyle sits on the landing adjacent to Sallie's door.)*

SALLIE
You're a causal guy Ly

LYLE
A causal guy

SALLIE
You're such a causal guy Ly

LYLE
As opposed to what

SALLIE
Me

LYLE
You don't believe in cause Sallie

SALLIE
Are you calling me irrational

LYLE
I worry about what's there Sallie

SALLIE
I worry about what's not here Lyle I mean
there

*(Sallie slips her fingers under the door and wiggles them. Lyle turns
suddenly and addresses Sallie's fingers.)*

LYLE
You know what you do You
hold forth on subjects Sallie
you neither fully understand nor
are completely ignorant of and
I invest belief in these flambéed theories and
conclusions this this
semi-enlightened limbo of yours this this
no-cigar sagacity only
to be rudely awakened at
inopportune social junctures I
do not like to be awakened rudely at
inopportune social junctures Sallie I
do not like it one bit

(Sallie's fingers stop wiggling and start pointing.)

SALLIE
There is little these days Lyle that you
like one bit In fact I dare
you Lyle to name one thing these days that you
like one bit whereas I on the other hand
like all too many things exactly
and no more than
one bit

LYLE
You are cranky Sallie because your
dissertation has proved a difficult
birth
You are a cranky Sallie

SALLIE
Don't apply baby metaphors to artistic
endeavor Lyle not in my
building's stairwell

LYLE
Your fear of unfortunate
phrases is ruining our relationship
Sallie

SALLIE
What is ruining our
relationship Lyle is your habit of
showing up at my door looking
skinny and appalled

LYLE
I'm not at all
skinny

SALLIE
You got any gum on ya

LYLE
Yeah

(Lyle slides a piece of gum under the door. Lyle and Sallie chew.)

JEN
What does that mean complicated in a fun way Like
kooky Like kooky with a "c"

KARL
I don't want to talk about inane things

JEN
Inanity is plucky honey There's something to be said for that

KARL
I brought you garbage for
God's sake

JEN
It's too late for
garbage

KARL
You need to reason with
those academics

JEN
Ha Anyway
I've tried

KARL
I doubt it

JEN
Your doubt is simple and idiomatic
Karl you are lucky

KARL
I have no coat I
am not lucky
I brought you garbage
and lots
of it
Excellent garbage
I don't deserve this
treatment

JEN
Basically
you have had the misfortune to
fall at the end of a long
line of ill-suitors who

together comprise my relationship history
faulty fellows and handsome
letdowns who were full-fledged
dullards and rascals by turn

KARL
I blame myself

JEN
Self-flagellation is icky and
unresourceful Karl

KARL
All right I blame you

JEN
Oh

(Slight pause.)

KARL
Did you call me honey before

JEN
Um hmm

(Sallie and Lyle are still chewing.)

SALLIE
I did secretly want to sleep with The Housesitter

LYLE
What

SALLIE
I want to sleep with a lot of people I'll
never sleep with
I mean I
picture myself with one person but then I catch sight of
all the rest of humanity
Sometimes I walk down the street and think

122

I won't have you and I
won't have you and I
won't have you and
it's a little sad really and it's
strange because sometimes I even mourn that I
won't have the people I'm not even attracted
to Whoever said life is short sure was correct

LYLE
You think Life Is Short is an attributable quote

SALLIE
Everything is attributable Lyle Why do you think I have
such a headache all the
time

LYLE
Sallie

SALLIE
and when I'm not walking around feeling stupid about my shame-
ful life and when I'm not walking around averting my eyes I'm
walking around feeling ripped off Don't you walk around feeling
ripped off Lyle

LYLE
I feel lucky Sallie

SALLIE
You feel yuchy Lyle

LYLE
Lucky

SALLIE
Yuchy how

LYLE
Lllucky lllucky

SALLIE
Lucky
you do

LYLE
I do

SALLIE
You do

LYLE
I do

SALLIE
You do

LYLE
I do
I do
I do

(They chew. Pause. Then everybody sings:)

JEN
WHY NOT TAKE OFF YOUR HAIR SHIRT
AND STAY A WHILE

SALLIE
I'D NEVER WAKE YOU ON PURPOSE

LYLE
THAT WOULD BE GUILE

SALLIE
SLEEP IS SACRED

JEN and SALLIE
SLEEP IS SACRED
SLEEP IS A SACRED THING

KARL
MY GUMPTION APPEARS

JEN
TO HAVE BEEN ELSEWHERE SHIPPED

KARL
IN A WORLD THAT WORSHIPS PRINT
YOU DREAM IN SCRIPT

LYLE
SCRIPT IS SACRED

JEN and LYLE
SCRIPT IS SACRED

JEN
SCRIPT IS A SACRED THING

LYLE
LISTEN TO THIS
AND MAKE IT YOUR MANTRA

LYLE and KARL
PEACE WILL ALWAYS
COME BACK TO HAUNT YA

SALLIE
I'D NEVER WAKE YOU ON PURPOSE
MY VOW REMAINS

KARL
IT IS MY HUMAN NATURE
TO LOVE WHAT'S LEFT

SALLIE
IF ONE COULD ONLY REFRAIN

SALLIE and JEN
FROM ONE'S REFRAIN

LYLE
SOMETIMES SMALL POTATOES

LYLE and KARL
TASTE THE BEST

JEN
POTATOES ARE SACRED
POTATOES ARE SACRED

SALLIE
POTATOES ARE A SACRED

(And then, after a moment, Jen and Sallie open their doors. And then, after another moment, Lyle enters Sallie's apartment, tentatively, while Karl descends the stairs and exits the building.)

End of Play

PROPERTY LIST

Light bulbs (SALLIE)
Dissertation in manuscript, pen (SALLIE)
Phone (JEN)
Cassette tape player, cassettes (JEN)
Suitcase, bag of trash containing cassette player, tapes (JEN)
Sharpie marker, label (JEN)
Phone (SALLIE, JEN)
Small rock (LYLE)
Binoculars (SALLIE)
Box of garbage (JEN)
Pen (SALLIE)
Chewing gum (KARL, LYLE)

SOUND EFFECTS

Buzz (to get into an apartment building)
Door buzzer (the sound of a door being released)
Breathing
Four tape-recorded excerpts from a cassette tape
Phone ring
Call waiting sound

NEW PLAYS

★ **THE EXONERATED by Jessica Blank and Erik Jensen.** Six interwoven stories paint a picture of an American criminal justice system gone horribly wrong and six brave souls who persevered to survive it. "The #1 play of the year...intense and deeply affecting..." –*NY Times.* "Riveting. Simple, honest storytelling that demands reflection." –*A.P.* "Artful and moving...pays tribute to the resilience of human hearts and minds." –*Variety.* "Stark...riveting...cunningly orchestrated." –*The New Yorker.* "Hard-hitting, powerful, and socially relevant." –*Hollywood Reporter.* [7M, 3W] ISBN: 0-8222-1946-8

★ **STRING FEVER by Jacquelyn Reingold.** Lily juggles the big issues: turning forty, artificial insemination and the elusive scientific Theory of Everything in this Off-Broadway comedy hit. "Applies the elusive rules of string theory to the conundrums of one woman's love life. Think *Sex and the City* meets *Copenhagen.*" –*NY Times.* "A funny offbeat and touching look at relationships...an appealing romantic comedy populated by oddball characters." –*NY Daily News.* "Where kooky, zany, and madcap meet...whimsically winsome." –*NY Magazine.* "STRING FEVER will have audience members happily stringing along." –*TheaterMania.com.* "Reingold's language is surprising, inventive, and unique." –*nytheatre.com.* "...[a] whimsical comic voice." –*Time Out.* [3M, 3W (doubling)] ISBN: 0-8222-1952-2

★ **DEBBIE DOES DALLAS adapted by Erica Schmidt, composed by Andrew Sherman, conceived by Susan L. Schwartz.** A modern morality tale told as a comic musical of tragic proportions as the classic film is brought to the stage. "A scream! A saucy, tongue-in-cheek romp." –*The New Yorker.* "Hilarious! DEBBIE manages to have it all: beauty, brains and a great sense of humor!" –*Time Out.* "Shamelessly silly, shrewdly self-aware and proud of being naughty. Great fun!" –*NY Times.* "Racy and raucous, a lighthearted, fast-paced thoroughly engaging and hilarious send-up." –*NY Daily News.* [3M, 5W] ISBN: 0-8222-1955-7

★ **THE MYSTERY PLAYS by Roberto Aguirre-Sacasa.** Two interrelated one acts, loosely based on the tradition of the medieval mystery plays. "... stylish, spine-tingling...Mr. Aguirre-Sacasa uses standard tricks of horror stories, borrowing liberally from masters like Kafka, Lovecraft, Hitchcock...But his mastery of the genre is his own...irresistible." –*NY Times.* "Undaunted by the special-effects limitations of theatre, playwright and *Marvel* comic-book writer Roberto Aguirre-Sacasa maps out some creepy twilight zones in THE MYSTERY PLAYS, an engaging, related pair of one acts...The theatre may rarely deliver shocks equivalent to, say, *Dawn of the Dead*, but Aguirre-Sacasa's work is fine compensation." –*Time Out.* [4M, 2W] ISBN: 0-8222-2038-5

★ **THE JOURNALS OF MIHAIL SEBASTIAN by David Auburn.** This epic one-man play spans eight tumultuous years and opens a uniquely personal window on the Romanian Holocaust and the Second World War. "Powerful." –*NY Times.* "[THE JOURNALS OF MIHAIL SEBASTIAN] allows us to glimpse the idiosyncratic effects of that awful history on one intelligent, pragmatic, recognizably real man..." –*NY Newsday.* [3M, 5W] ISBN: 0-8222-2006-7

★ **LIVING OUT by Lisa Loomer.** The story of the complicated relationship between a Salvadoran nanny and the Anglo lawyer she works for. "A stellar new play. Searingly funny." –*The New Yorker.* "Both generous and merciless, equally enjoyable and disturbing." –*NY Newsday.* "A bitingly funny new comedy. The plight of working mothers is explored from two pointedly contrasting perspectives in this sympathetic, sensitive new play." –*Variety.* [2M, 6W] ISBN: 0-8222-1994-8

DRAMATISTS PLAY SERVICE, INC.
440 Park Avenue South, New York, NY 10016 212-683-8960 Fax 212-213-1539
postmaster@dramatists.com www.dramatists.com

NEW PLAYS

★ **MATCH by Stephen Belber.** Mike and Lisa Davis interview a dancer and choreographer about his life, but it is soon evident that their agenda will either ruin or inspire them—and definitely change their lives forever. "Prolific laughs and ear-to-ear smiles." *–NY Magazine.* "Uproariously funny, deeply moving, enthralling theater. Stephen Belber's MATCH has great beauty and tenderness, and abounds in wit." *–NY Daily News.* "Three and a half out of four stars." *–USA Today.* "A theatrical steeplechase that leads straight from outrageous bitchery to unadorned, heartfelt emotion." *–Wall Street Journal.* [2M, 1W] ISBN: 0-8222-2020-2

★ **HANK WILLIAMS: LOST HIGHWAY by Randal Myler and Mark Harelik.** The story of the beloved and volatile country-music legend Hank Williams, featuring twenty-five of his most unforgettable songs. "[LOST HIGHWAY has] the exhilarating feeling of Williams on stage in a particular night...serves up classic country with the edges raw and the energy hot...By the end of the play, you've traveled on a profound emotional journey: LOST HIGHWAY transports its audience and communicates the inspiring message of the beauty and richness of Williams' songs...forceful, clear-eyed, moving, impressive." *–Rolling Stone.* "...honors a very particular musical talent with care and energy... smart, sweet, poignant." *–NY Times.* [7M, 3W] ISBN: 0-8222-1985-9

★ **THE STORY by Tracey Scott Wilson.** An ambitious black newspaper reporter goes against her editor to investigate a murder and finds the *best* story...but at what cost? "A singular new voice...deeply emotional, deeply intellectual, and deeply musical..." *–The New Yorker.* "...a conscientious and absorbing new drama..." *–NY Times.* "...a riveting, tough-minded drama about race, reporting and the truth..." *–A.P.* "... a stylish, attention-holding script that ends on a chilling note that will leave viewers with much to talk about." *–Curtain Up.* [2M, 7W (doubling, flexible casting)] ISBN: 0-8222-1998-0

★ **OUR LADY OF 121st STREET by Stephen Adly Guirgis.** The body of Sister Rose, beloved Harlem nun, has been stolen, reuniting a group of life-challenged childhood friends who square off as they wait for her return. "A scorching and dark new comedy... Mr. Guirgis has one of the finest imaginations for dialogue to come along in years." *–NY Times.* "Stephen Guirgis may be the best playwright in America under forty." *–NY Magazine.* [8M, 4W] ISBN: 0-8222-1965-4

★ **HOLLYWOOD ARMS by Carrie Hamilton and Carol Burnett.** The coming-of-age story of a dreamer who manages to escape her bleak life and follow her romantic ambitions to stardom. Based on Carol Burnett's bestselling autobiography, *One More Time.* "...pure theatre and pure entertainment..." *–Talkin' Broadway.* "...a warm, fuzzy evening of theatre." *–BrodwayBeat.com.* "...chuckles and smiles of recognition or surprise flow naturally...a remarkable slice of life." *–TheatreScene.net.* [5M, 5W, 1 girl] ISBN: 0-8222-1959-X

★ **INVENTING VAN GOGH by Steven Dietz.** A haunting and hallucinatory drama about the making of art, the obsession to create and the fine line that separates truth from myth. "Like a van Gogh painting, Dietz's story is a gorgeous example of excess—one that remakes reality with broad, well-chosen brush strokes. At evening's end, we're left with the author's resounding opinions on art and artifice, and provoked by his constant query into which is greater: van Gogh's art or his violent myth." *–Phoenix New Times.* "Dietz's writing is never simple. It is always brilliant. Shaded, compressed, direct, lucid—he frames his subject with a remarkable understanding of painting as a physical experience." *–Tucson Citizen.* [4M, 1W] ISBN: 0-8222-1954-9

DRAMATISTS PLAY SERVICE, INC.
440 Park Avenue South, New York, NY 10016 212-683-8960 Fax 212-213-1539
postmaster@dramatists.com www.dramatists.com

NEW PLAYS

★ **INTIMATE APPAREL by Lynn Nottage.** The moving and lyrical story of a turn-of-the-century black seamstress whose gifted hands and sewing machine are the tools she uses to fashion her dreams from the whole cloth of her life's experiences. "...Nottage's play has a delicacy and eloquence that seem absolutely right for the time she is depicting..." *–NY Daily News.* "...thoughtful, affecting...The play offers poignant commentary on an era when the cut and color of one's dress—and of course, skin—determined whom one could and could not marry, sleep with, even talk to in public." *–Variety.* [2M, 4W] ISBN: 0-8222-2009-1

★ **BROOKLYN BOY by Donald Margulies.** A witty and insightful look at what happens to a writer when his novel hits the bestseller list. "The characters are beautifully drawn, the dialogue sparkles..." *–nytheatre.com.* "Few playwrights have the mastery to smartly investigate so much through a laugh-out-loud comedy that combines the vintage subject matter of successful writer-returning-to-ethnic-roots with the familiar mid-life crisis." *–Show Business Weekly.* [4M, 3W] ISBN: 0-8222-2074-1

★ **CROWNS by Regina Taylor.** Hats become a springboard for an exploration of black history and identity in this celebratory musical play. "Taylor pulls off a Hat Trick: She scores thrice, turning CROWNS into an artful amalgamation of oral history, fashion show, and musical theater..." *–TheatreMania.com.* "...wholly theatrical...Ms. Taylor has created a show that seems to arise out of spontaneous combustion, as if a bevy of department-store customers simultaneously decided to stage a revival meeting in the changing room." *–NY Times.* [1M, 6W (2 musicians)] ISBN: 0-8222-1963-8

★ **EXITS AND ENTRANCES by Athol Fugard.** The story of a relationship between a young playwright on the threshold of his career and an aging actor who has reached the end of his. "[Fugard] can say more with a single line than most playwrights convey in an entire script...Paraphrasing the title, it's safe to say this drama, making its memorable entrance into our consciousness, is unlikely to exit as long as a theater exists for exceptional work." *–Variety.* "A thought-provoking, elegant and engrossing new play..." *–Hollywood Reporter.* [2M] ISBN: 0-8222-2041-5

★ **BUG by Tracy Letts.** A thriller featuring a pair of star-crossed lovers in an Oklahoma City motel facing a bug invasion, paranoia, conspiracy theories and twisted psychological motives. "...obscenely exciting...top-flight craftsmanship. Buckle up and brace yourself..." *–NY Times.* "...[a] thoroughly outrageous and thoroughly entertaining play...the possibility of enemies, real and imagined, to squash has never been more theatrical." *–A.P.* [3M, 2W] ISBN: 0-8222-2016-4

★ **THOM PAIN (BASED ON NOTHING) by Will Eno.** An ordinary man muses on childhood, yearning, disappointment and loss, as he draws the audience into his last-ditch plea for empathy and enlightenment. "It's one of those treasured nights in the theater—treasured nights anywhere, for that matter—that can leave you both breathless with exhilaration and...in a puddle of tears." *–NY Times.* "Eno's words...are familiar, but proffered in a way that is constantly contradictory to our expectations. Beckett is certainly among his literary ancestors." *–nytheatre.com.* [1M] ISBN: 0-8222-2076-8

★ **THE LONG CHRISTMAS RIDE HOME by Paula Vogel.** Past, present and future collide on a snowy Christmas Eve for a troubled family of five. "...[a] lovely and hauntingly original family drama...a work that breathes so much life into the theater." *–Time Out.* "...[a] delicate visual feast..." *–NY Times.* "...brutal and lovely...the overall effect is magical." *–NY Newsday.* [3M, 3W] ISBN: 0-8222-2003-2

DRAMATISTS PLAY SERVICE, INC.
440 Park Avenue South, New York, NY 10016 212-683-8960 Fax 212-213-1539
postmaster@dramatists.com www.dramatists.com